HOW LONG IS NOT LONG?

A Personal Journey

DAPHNE GLOAG

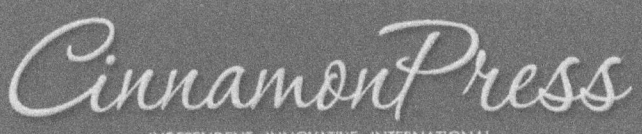

Published by Cinnamon Press
Meirion House
Tanygrisiau
Blaenau Ffestiniog
Gwynedd, LL41 3SU
www.cinnamonpress.com

The right of Daphne Gloag to be identified as author of this work has been asserted by her in accordance with the Copyright, Designs and Patent Act 1988. Copyright © 2018 Daphne Gloag.
ISBN: 978-1 78864-024-4
British Library Cataloguing in Publication Data. A CIP record for this book can be obtained from the British Library.
All rights reserved. No part of this publication may be reproduced, stored in a retrieval system, or transmitted in any form or by any means, electronic, mechanical, photocopying, recording or otherwise, without the prior written permission of the publishers. This book may not be lent, hired out, resold or otherwise disposed of by way of trade in any form of binding or cover other than that in which it is published, without the prior consent of the publishers.

Designed and typeset in Palatino by Cinnamon Press.
Cover design by Adam Craig.
Printed in Poland
Cinnamon Press is represented in the UK by Inpress Ltd and in Wales by the Welsh Books Council

Acknowledgements

A version of this poem sequence was commended in the Second Light long poem competition, and extracts have been published in *ARTEMISpoetry*.

I am most grateful to Dr Paul Murdin for his advice on cosmological aspects of the sequence. I have had valuable comments and helpful discussion from members of the Pitshanger Poets weekly workshop and from Carol DeVaughn, Joan Goodall, and Pete Marshall. Jan Fortune has given me unfailing skilled help and friendly support, for which I am immensely grateful.

Previous publications have been *Diversities of Silence* from Brentham Press (1994) and from Cinnamon Press *A Compression of Distances* (2009) and *Beginnings and Other Poems* (2013).

Contents

Prelude

On liking time   7

What is Time?

Beginning   9
But is there such a thing as time?   10
Space and time at Canovium Roman Fort   11
How long is not long?   12
Like a book   13
Time leaping   14
Tick tick   15
Where has the time gone?   16
Time flies   17
The giant sequoia   18
Burial   19
Will time end?   20

Past, Present, Future

The three   21
Not like a road   22
Footprints in the sand   23
Winters   24
Our Now   25
How long is Now?   26
Like starlings in the evening sky   27
The fires of Now   28
Window   29
Orbiting the sun   30

Notes   31

In memory of Peter, who inhabited time with me

How long is not long?
A personal journey

See notes on p.31

Prelude

On liking time

The question made no sense. Someone asked
what we did to pass time. Why
should we want to pass time, leave it behind?
It stayed beside us, kept us company. We
      had no wish to pass on.
        We liked time.

We often talked about saving time. What
would we do if it came to a bad end? Or if
it just quietly disappeared, or was miserly
with its many favours? We wanted more,
        always more.

But sometimes we wasted time, playing games
with words instead of getting supper. The risk
was throwing it out as rubbish. Would we ever
find it then? We could not afford
      to lose it for
      we liked time.

One day we lost time, took
a wrong turning on our way to the station.
Nothing like that here, they said; but at last
we found it in lost property safe and sound.
        We breathed again.

How could anyone think of beating time?
What use to keep time then? We
wanted of course to keep it, not beaten
black and blue, not cowering in a corner
        but as a friend.
        We liked time.

Someone spoke of killing time. He said
it was too much for him. Did it deserve
so violent an end? And was there anything
to take its place? We worried. We had no wish
              to view its coffin.

Together we would make time: we
had a good recipe, good ingredients –
words in the right proportion, the right amount
of silence, seasoning with laughter.
        So it sang for us.
        We loved time.

What Is Time?

Beginning

We could not understand
      that big bang of time and space
      which had no before

We only knew
      narratives of our dark
      our light

We only knew
      vocabularies of years
      of days imprinted on sky

              possibilities of time

But is there such a thing as time?

The light and the black
the crescent and the circle
the green and the brown
    come round and round

Time time its lines and circles
time time its paths and journeys
time time its river and ocean
    flow over me

If I were time I'd sing a song
tick tock tick tock my tune
But what if time is no more than our clock
    what if time could not be my song?

Space and time at Canovium Roman Fort

Trajectories, dimensions everywhere.
                                            I look down
                                       from the present
                                        beyond stones,
                              beyond bits of centuries,
              to the river, its present, its past.
                                                    Time
                                        tumbling down

from this churchyard where I stand now
to lives lived in the Roman fort below
when it guarded the river crossing.

                       Coordinates hold their precisions.
Down the hillside
              to the left a little
                  then straight ahead,
two thousand years ago the moment
when an adventurous child
                                                treads
                                     barefoot on tile,
                                toes press into clay
                                      not yet set,
            imprint of time and space.
Absent child, lost footsteps,
                    time
            carried to today's light.

How long is not long?

The train had been late, but no matter:
time stretched ahead of us. The lake
was our destination, trees and reflections
of trees, blue of sky…reality
and dream. But the maples' autumn colour,
the dream of trees, would not last long.
    How long was not long?

We were close, our bodies were joined
together. We paddled in ice-cold water,
made joint ripples, dents
in space-time. So would our time
pass more slowly, we wondered,
would we feel extra time was granted
    for the dream?

Like a book

Words had been all around us, and we'd seized them
joyfully. Some were wearing
funny hats, or were dressed in black:
words for all occasions. They put themselves

in a book of stories of our years,
in a library of many stories.
I hoped to undo the pages, allow
the words to go anywhere they pleased

and welcome new words in. But something
held the pages, the words in just that order.
Trying to turn the pages back,
rewrite the last sentence of his life,

I heard the words laugh at me.

Time leaping

Midnight heavy with that extra second,
time multiplied. Always
we craved for more, were greedy for time.
But that last midnight when one second
turned into two he was not here.
His time was zero…zero doubled
    a harsh arithmetic.

In our years of midnights extra seconds
leapt into the night unseen:
donated moments for our bodies
to share warmth, for words, our currency,
to make extra phrases. But all our days
had seconds, hours leaping, dancing
    in the austerities of time.

Tick tick

Tick tick tick it goes: after the next tick
another will follow
and another and another,
a line of ticks, no gaps, no end,
marching, marching, I march. Pushed. Shoved. I go on marching

until one day
        I run away
                close my ears
                        to ticks and fears

                      I find a river
                    its water clear
                winding at leisure
              neither fast nor slow
            sun's light on the water
            river's voice a whisper

            Tick tick does not exist
                the river flows

Where has the time gone?

It's missing again, he said.
Where has it gone?
                    This was serious:
                we could not afford
                 to lose track of it,
              we did not want to say
                   I haven't time.

We searched
                                         in the kitchen,
                                      in our rucksacks
                             in our wallets, notebooks,
                                           in our bed.

At last
                we found it
                in our heads
            where the traffic was heaviest,
                    jostled,
                crowded out.

We took it by the hand
                                   to a green quiet place
not wanting it to go
                                             for ever.

Time flies

It flew
                                  in the garden
it flew
                                                       in the house
it flew
                                                        everywhere
                       it sang
hours   days
                       all full
                                             all full of flying

We willed it not
                                                        to fly away

but fly away
it did
                                                            finally
                                                           fading

into dark

The giant sequoia

It was a kind of pilgrimage we made
together, to meet a giant sequoia standing
at the top of a hill like a climax. Over three millennia
it had grown towards the sky. I said, *It is not
years of a tree we're celebrating here,
it is the years of time.* We stood inside
the trunk as if it were a house. But he said, *The more
the years pile up the nearer it comes to the end
of time, its time.* We were quiet, feeling the fear
for that great trunk no longer making statements
on the sky but lying across the road
of time, feeling too the fear for ourselves
of what would fall across our time, the road
        blocked by a stop sign.

Burial

Piled up stones, rocks, centuries...
buzzards soar above days;
sheep graze, eating away hours.
Bodies buried beneath years
have gone from their stone chambers
leaving
emptiness between the granite
and the granite,
leaving time behind,
just as he
left time behind with me,
just as I
at last will have days, years
severed from me.

Will time end?

It was beautiful, the landscape,
crowded with changes of sun and season,
                no horizon.
Always it was expanding;
trees became scattered,
         absent,
summer and winter were further and further
            apart.
Would summer never
            come?

Is Never an event?
Does Nothing make a landscape?

I dreamed about a choir singing.
I was inside the music, admired
          its harmonies.
I was there
          when distances
came between
          the singers,
                    distances growing,
when the sound of a voice
          became
                a rare
                          event,
          became
                                silence,

in the way the words of his life became more and more
sparse, no longer holding hands
          across time's distances,
              finally
                    turning into
                                silence.

Past, Present, Future

The three

They're always quarrelling...disagreements
about who should dominate and have his say,
or keep quiet. Should they be left
to get on with it or should one or other
be favoured? And they chatter so,
on and on!
                Now sees himself
as ringleader yet he so easily
lets himself be overruled. But in the end
he has his way – the others are mere shadows,
no match for him. One of them may lie.
And the other—I wonder sometimes
if he exists at all.
                Well, I wouldn't be without them.
But I should spend more time in the company of Now,
not let myself be sidetracked by the other two.
                He makes me real.

Not like a road

Just a bit of fun it was
that day when I was ten, walking
backwards. The road ahead getting longer,
always longer…distance stretching.
I turn to face backwards still
but it's not a road I see, tidy
rows of houses, numbers advancing
from 1 and 2 as if they were days
on a calendar.

The past is a wood   not always
        a clear path

There are oak birch beech trees
        pines here and there
              sometimes dense
like events of a crowded day
        sometimes with spaces
   letting   sun   through
     and rain

There's interlacing of branches
    they make patterns
and leaves are various
      like speech like words
          but the far edge of the wood
        is misty   trees
       hard
         to make out

But the wood of love I remember always
     we walked there   counted
       magpies in those trees
            One for sorrow he'd say
              two for joy

Footprints in the sand

A photograph

High tide has come, has passed.
Oyster catchers wait for sand
their grazing ground, their cries
    part of the blue.

Marram grass on the dunes,
backs to the west, obedient
like good soldiers, obedient
    to the wind...

shadows of grass, of hummocks
of sand, shadows of moments.
Feet have pressed time into sand
    beyond tide's reach,

footprints of father, mother on sand
that's dry and warm under the sun,
warm for a child's bare feet
    as she waits for tides.

Winters

Past winters, the year's cold
descending, decisive statement…we wrapped
words round each other, counted
redwings carrying winter with them.
Snow falling without emphasis,
it needed none. Melted by words,
    warmth of words.

So round and round our winters came.
Time was lived in…more, always more.
Bare branches allowed the sky
to share its changes. Wind raced
through moments, through darkness of winter, words
heaped up, always there, fires
    igniting the season.

This present winter has no occasions
of redwings, no words for their flight.
No counting is needed now.
I look for words to support the sky,
new words of the season, I watch
frost melting on car roofs
    in spite of cold.

Searching for sky, stories, edifice
of words I live through moments, changes.
Not empty air, not brief glimpses
of memory, but solid, comfortable,
this winter's for holding and cherishing, for loading
with treasure, with the strangeness of being:
    gifts of Now.

Our Now

Dark hillside, dark folding up light.
The magic apple tree
invisible. *Is this*, I said,
how the future will end?
      But *Now   Now*
he whispered as he gently placed Now
in the space we shared, the light
of a comet playing games with the dark.
      Now wobbled a little.
Be careful, I said. *Look at the dark sky.*
Are there no magic apples for us?
      Then we saw one landing softly
on top of Now.

How long is Now?

You have to go straight to the point,
says the gannet.
                              Now.

But how long is Now? I say.
He does not reply.
                              He's diving in
                                    fast
                              from a height
                              for his fish.

It's a vertical dive,
the shortest line
between two points.

                                                        He doesn't mess about,
                              takes
                        no liberties with
                              Now.
                           The fish
                  is plump, satisfying, fills
                          the moment.
But even as he eats,
I see a horse galloping
towards rocks and mists of mountains,
towards distances, carrying away
Now.

Like starlings in the evening sky

        They won't go on for ever, he'd say.
                And they didn't
                    for him.
For me meanwhile moments come
over and over.
                They flow
           like a flock of starlings
             in the evening sky
             flying on and on

                            as if for ever.

The fires of Now

What would you like for supper today? I said.
It was a moment like any other,
ablaze with Now, and the plodding tread
of necessity could not quench for us
    its fire.

Stairs led to rooms where other fires would light
moments yet to be explored. We started
to climb the stairs, found again the brilliance
of fire. But ahead the staircase would end in mid air,
    broken.

Window

A dark pile of rocks, years: once
it was a wall of a house sheltering
minutes, sheltering hours; the hole at its centre,

a window once, gave light to lives.
I peer through that empty space looking
for views of my life. Is there is ruin of rock,

crumbling years, grass with earth showing through?
But now I see nothing beyond the space
except a blue exuberance of light,

the lit sky of the present moment.

Orbiting the sun

And there it was hanging in the dark
as I opened the door, lighting the years
of its journey round the sun, lighting
    the years carved from time.

What happens, he said once, *when a comet
passes the sun? Might it disintegrate,
or else vanish into darkness? Lose
    the possibility of light?*

Now when I open the door, interrogating
the dark he's become a part of, I ask questions
of my comet. Does it show signs of dimming,
    or will it shine strongly

on years full of circumstance, of shapes
captured from time? How many orbits will it make,
coaxing moments from darkness, before it loses
    the possibilities of time?

But now it is still making a difference to the dark.

Notes

9   Beginning
Both space and time are thought to have come into existence with the big bang 13.8 billion years ago.

10   But is there such a thing as time?
Not all scientists believe that time exists.

11   Space and time at Canovium Roman Fort
This Roman fort (built around AD 77-8) is in north Wales near the mouth of the River Conwy. It was extended to include a civilian settlement in the second century. The tile referred to is in Llandudno Museum.

12   How long is not long?
The end of this poem is a non-serious application of relativity theory: close to a massive object such as the earth—or, in the fanciful imagery of the poem, the conjunction of two bodies—time and space are warped or dented and durations are extended according to general relativity.

14   Time leaping
Because of irregularities in the earth's rotation an extra second, a leap second, is occasionally inserted into our time derived from atomic clocks to preserve its relation to solar time.

20   Will time end?
Space-time is thought to be expanding, implying that the objects and events it holds will move apart, leading ultimately, it is argued, to empty darkness and silence (though other scenarios have been proposed) and the non-existence of time.

25   Our Now
The Magic Apple Tree is a painting by Samuel Palmer.

www.ingramcontent.com/pod-product-compliance
Lightning Source LLC
Chambersburg PA
CBHW031509040426
42444CB00007B/1266